Simple Air Fryer Recipes

Learn How to Cook Delicious, Low-Fat Recipes with Your Air Fryer on a Budget

Linda Wang

© Copyright 2021 by Linda Wang - All rights reserved.

The content contained within this book may not be reproduced, duplicated or transmitted without direct written permission from the author or the publisher.
Under no circumstances will any blame or legal responsibility be held against the publisher, or author, for any damages, reparation, or monetary loss due to the information contained within this book. Either directly or indirectly.

Legal Notice:
This book is copyright protected. This book is only for personal use. You cannot amend, distribute, sell, use, quote or paraphrase any part, or the content within this book, without the consent of the author or publisher.

Disclaimer Notice:
Please note the information contained within this document is for educational and entertainment purposes only. All effort has been executed to present accurate, up to date, and reliable, complete information. No warranties of any kind are declared or implied. Readers acknowledge that the author is not engaging in the rendering of legal, financial, medical or professional advice. The content within this book has been derived from various sources. Please consult a licensed professional before attempting any techniques outlined in this book.
By reading this document, the reader agrees that under no circumstances is the author responsible for any losses, direct or indirect, which are incurred as a result of the use of information contained within this document, including, but not limited to, — errors, omissions, or inaccuracies.

TABLE OF CONTENTS

INTRODUCTION 1

Avocado Cauliflower Toast 5

Blackberries Bowls 7

Creamy Parsley Soufflé 8

Fennel and Tomato Stew 10

Buttery Artichokes 12

Turkey and Mushroom Stew 14

Zucchini Stew 16

Zucchini and Cauliflower Stew 18

Pita Bread Cheese Pizza 20

Tasty Portabella Pizza 21

Spinach and Artichokes Sauté 23

Cheesy Garlic Biscuits 24

Scrambled Eggs with Tomato and Spinach 26

Lemony Flounder Fillets 28

Garlic Lemon Shrimp 30

E-Z Catfish 32

Salmon Croquettes 33

Peas and Cod Fillets 35

Sea Bass Paella 37

Hawaiian Salmon Recipe 39

Mussels Bowls	41
Devil Chicken	42
Citrus Turkey Legs	44
Delightful Turkey Wings	46
Chicken and Peppercorns	48
Garlic Chicken	49
Chicken Fried Rice	51
Chicken Drumsticks	53
Bacon Wrapped Herb Chicken	55
Lamb Stew	57
Herbed Lamb Chops	59
Veggie Stuffed Beef Rolls	61
Roasted Lamb	63
Chinese Style Beef	65
Lamb and Beans	66
Simple Stuffed Tomatoes	68
Herbed Veggies Combo	70
Couscous Stuffed Tomatoes	72
Tofu with Veggies	74
Cheese Stuffed Mushrooms	77
Air fryer Mediterranean Lentil and Collard Soup	79
Air fryer Bean Soup	81
Cheese and Leeks Dip	83

Mozzarella Sticks 85

Sunflower Seeds Bread 87

Spiced Soy Curls 89

Peanut Butter Cookies 91

Coffee Cheesecakes Recipe 93

Ginger Cookies 96

Cherry-Choco Bars 98

NOTES 100

INTRODUCTION

An Air Fryer is a magic revolutionized kitchen appliance that helps you fry with less or even no oil at all. This kind of product applies Rapid Air technology, which offers a new way to fry with less oil. This new invention cooks food through the circulation of superheated air and generates 80% low-fat food. Although the food is fried with less oil, you don't need to worry as the food processed by the Air Fryer still has the same taste like the food fried using the deep-frying method.

This technology uses a superheated element, which radiates heat close to the food and an exhaust fan in its lid to circulate airflow. An Air Fryer ensures that the food processed is cooked completely. The exhaust fan located at the top of the cooking chamber helps the food get the same heating temperature in every part quickly, resulting in a cooked food of better and healthier quality. Besides, cooking with an Air Fryer is also suitable for those individuals which are too busy or do not have enough time. For example, an Air Fryer only needs half a spoonful of oil and takes 10 minutes to serve a medium bowl of crispy French fries.

In addition to serving healthier food, an Air Fryer also provides some other benefits to you. Since an Air Fryer helps you fry using less oil or without oil for some kind of food, it automatically reduces the fat and cholesterol content in food. Indeed, no one will refuse to enjoy fried food without worrying about the greasy and fat content. Having fried food with no guilt is one of the pleasures of life. Besides having low fat and cholesterol, you save some amount of money by consuming oil sparingly, which can be used for other needs. An Air Fryer also can reheat your food. Sometimes, when you have fried leftover and you reheat it, it will usually serve reheated greasy food with some addition of unhealthy reuse oil. Undoubtedly, the saturated fat in the fried food gets worse because of this process. An Air Fryer helps you reheat your food without being afraid of extra oils that the food may absorb. Fried bananas, fish and chips, nuggets, or even fried chicken can be reheated to become as warm and crispy as they were before by using an Air Fryer.

Some people may think that spending some amount of money to buy a fryer is wasteful. I dare to say that they are wrong because an Air Fryer is not only used to fry. It is a sophisticated multi-function appliance since it also helps you to roast chicken, make steak, grill fish, and even bake a cake. With a built-in air filter, an Air Fryer filters the air and saves your kitchen from smoke and grease.

An air Fryer is really a new innovative method of cooking. Grab it fast and welcome to a clean and healthy kitchen.

Avocado Cauliflower Toast

Preparation Time: 23 minutes

Servings: 2

Ingredients:

- 1 large egg.
- 1: 12-oz. steamer bag cauliflower
- ½ cup shredded mozzarella cheese
- 1 ripe medium avocado
- ½ tsp. garlic powder.
- ¼ tsp. ground black pepper

Directions:

1. Cook cauliflower according to package instructions. Remove from bag and place into cheesecloth or clean towel to remove excess moisture.
2. Place cauliflower into a large bowl and mix in egg and mozzarella. Cut a piece of parchment to fit your air fryer basket

3. Separate the cauliflower mixture into two and place it on the parchment in two mounds. Press out the cauliflower mounds into a ¼-inch-thick rectangle. Place the parchment into the air fryer basket.
4. Adjust the temperature to 400 Degrees F and set the timer for 8 minutes
5. Flip the cauliflower halfway through the cooking time
6. When the timer beeps, remove the parchment and allow the cauliflower to cool 5 minutes.
7. Cut open the avocado and remove the pit. Scoop out the inside, place it in a medium bowl and mash it with garlic powder and pepper. Spread onto the cauliflower.

Nutrition:

Calories: 278; Protein: 14.1g; Fiber: 8.2g; Fat: 15.6g; Carbs: 15.9g

Blackberries Bowls

Preparation Time: 20 minutes

Servings: 4

Ingredients:

- ½ cup blackberries
- 1 ½ cups coconut milk
- ½ cup coconut; shredded
- 2 tsp. stevia

Directions:

1. In your air fryer's pan, mix all the ingredients, stir, cover and cook at 360 °F for 15 minutes.
2. Divide into bowls and serve

Nutrition:

Calories: 171; Fat: 4g; Fiber: 2g; Carbs: 3g; Protein: 5g

Creamy Parsley Soufflé

Preparation Time: 5 minutes

Cooking Time: 10 minutes

Servings: 2

Ingredients:

- 2 eggs
- 1 tablespoon fresh parsley, chopped

- 2 tablespoons light cream
- 1 fresh red chili pepper, chopped
- Salt, to taste

Directions:

1. Preheat the Air fryer to 390 degrees F and grease 2 soufflé dishes.
2. Mix together all the ingredients in a bowl until well combined.
3. Transfer the mixture into prepared soufflé dishes and place in the Air fryer.
4. Cook for about 10 minutes and dish out to serve warm.

Nutrition:

Calories: 108, Fat: 9g, Carbs: 1.1g, Sugar: 0.5g, Protein: 6g, Sodium: 146mg

Fennel and Tomato Stew

Preparation Time: 25 minutes

Servings: 4

Ingredients:

- 2 fennel bulbs; shredded
- 1 red bell pepper; chopped.
- ½ cup chicken stock
- 2 tbsp. tomato puree
- 2 garlic cloves; minced
- 2 cups tomatoes; cubed
- 1 tsp. rosemary; dried
- 1 tsp. sweet paprika
- Salt and black pepper to taste.

Directions:

1. In a pan that fits your air fryer, mix all the ingredients, toss, introduce in the fryer and cook at 380 °F for 15 minutes
2. Divide the stew into bowls.

Nutrition:

Calories: 184; Fat: 7g; Fiber: 2g; Carbs: 3g; Protein: 8g

Buttery Artichokes

Preparation Time: 10 minutes

Cooking time: 20 minutes

Servings: 4

Ingredients:

- 4 artichokes, trimmed and halved
- 3 garlic cloves, minced

- 1 tablespoon olive oil
- 4 tablespoons butter, melted
- ¼ teaspoon cumin, ground
- 1 tablespoon lemon zest, grated
- Salt and black pepper to the taste

Directions:

1. In a bowl, combine the artichokes with the oil, garlic and the other ingredients, toss well and transfer them to the air fryer's basket.
2. Cook for 20 minutes at 370 degrees F, divide between plates and serve as a side dish.

Nutrition:

Calories 214, fat 5, fiber 8, carbs 12, protein 5

Turkey and Mushroom Stew

Preparation Time: 30 minutes

Servings: 4

Ingredients:

- 1 turkey breast, skinless, boneless; cubed and browned
- ½ lb. brown mushrooms; sliced

- ¼ cup tomato sauce
- 1 tbsp. parsley; chopped.
- Salt and black pepper to taste.

Directions:

1. In a pan that fits your air fryer, mix the turkey with the mushrooms, salt, pepper and tomato sauce, toss, introduce in the fryer and cook at 350 °F for 25 minutes
2. Divide into bowls and serve for lunch with parsley sprinkled on top.

Nutrition:

Calories: 220; Fat: 12g; Fiber: 2g; Carbs: 5g; Protein: 12g

Zucchini Stew

Preparation Time: 17 minutes

Servings: 4

Ingredients:

- 8 zucchinis, roughly cubed
- ¼ cup tomato sauce
- ½ tsp. basil; chopped.
- 1 tbsp. olive oil

- ¼ tsp. rosemary; dried
- Salt and black pepper to taste.

Directions:

1. Grease a pan that fits your air fryer with the oil, add all the ingredients, toss, introduce the pan in the fryer and cook at 350 °F for 12 minutes
2. Divide into bowls and serve.

Nutrition:

Calories: 200; Fat: 6g; Fiber: 2g; Carbs: 4g; Protein: 6g

Zucchini and Cauliflower Stew

Preparation Time: 25 minutes

Servings: 4

Ingredients:

- 1 cauliflower head, florets separated
- 1 ½ cups zucchinis; sliced
- 1 handful parsley leaves; chopped.
- 2 green onions; chopped.
- ½ cup tomato puree

- 1 tbsp. balsamic vinegar
- 1 tbsp. olive oil
- Salt and black pepper to taste.

Directions:

1. In a pan that fits your air fryer, mix the zucchinis with the rest of the ingredients except the parsley, toss, introduce the pan in the air fryer and cook at 380 °F for 20 minutes
2. Divide into bowls and serve for lunch with parsley sprinkled on top.

Nutrition:

Calories: 193; Fat: 5g; Fiber: 2g; Carbs: 4g; Protein: 7g

Pita Bread Cheese Pizza

Preparation Time: 15 minutes

Servings: 2

Ingredients:

- 1-piece Pita bread
- 1/2-pound Mozzarella cheese
- 1 tablespoon olive oil
- 2 tablespoon ketchup
- 1/3 cup sausage
- 1 teaspoon garlic powder

Directions:

1. Using a tablespoon spread ketchup over Pita bread.
2. Then; add sausage and cheese. Sprinkle with garlic powder and with 1 tablespoon olive oil.
3. Preheat the Air Fryer to 340 - degrees Fahrenheit and carefully transfer your pizza to a fryer basket. Cook for 6 minutes and enjoy your quick & easy pizza.

Tasty Portabella Pizza

Preparation Time: 15 minutes

Servings: 2

Ingredients:
- 3 portabella mushroom caps; cleaned and scooped
- 3 tablespoon olive oil
- 3 tablespoon mozzarella; shredded

- 3 tablespoon tomato sauce
- 12 slices pepperoni
- 1 pinch salt
- 1 pinch dried Italian seasonings

Directions:

1. Preheat the Air Fryer to 330 - degrees Fahrenheit.
2. On both sides of the portabella; drizzle oil and then season the inside with Italian seasonings and salt. Spread tomato sauce evenly over the mushroom and top with cheese.
3. Place the portabella into the cooking basket of the Air Fryer. Place pepperoni slices on top of the portabella pizza after 1 minute of cooking. Cook for 3 to 5 minutes.

Spinach and Artichokes Sauté

Preparation Time: 20 minutes

Servings: 4

Ingredients:

- 10 oz. artichoke hearts; halved
- 2 cups baby spinach
- ¼ cup veggie stock
- 3 garlic cloves
- 2 tsp. lime juice
- Salt and black pepper to taste.

Directions:

1. In a pan that fits your air fryer, mix all the ingredients, toss, introduce in the fryer and cook at 370 °F for 15 minutes
2. Divide between plates and serve as a side dish.

Nutrition:

Calories: 209; Fat: 6g; Fiber: 2g; Carbs: 4g; Protein: 8g

Cheesy Garlic Biscuits

Preparation Time: 17 minutes

Servings: 4

Ingredients:
- 1 large egg.
- 1 scallion, sliced
- ½ cup shredded sharp Cheddar cheese.
- ¼ cup unsalted butter; melted and divided
- ⅓ cup coconut flour
- ½ tsp. baking powder.
- ½ tsp. garlic powder.

Directions:
1. Take a large bowl, mix coconut flour, baking powder and garlic powder.
2. Stir in egg, half of the melted butter, Cheddar cheese and scallions. Pour the mixture into a 6-inch round baking pan. Place into the air fryer basket

3. Adjust the temperature to 320 Degrees F and set the timer for 12 minutes
4. To serve, remove from pan and allow to fully cool. Slice into four pieces and pour remaining melted butter over each.

Nutrition:

Calories: 218; Protein: 7.2g; Fiber: 3.4g; Fat: 16.9g; Carbs: 6.8g

Scrambled Eggs with Tomato and Spinach

Preparation Time: 15 minutes

Servings: 2

Ingredients:

- 2 tablespoons olive oil; melted
- 5 ounces fresh spinach; chopped
- four eggs; whisked

- 1 teaspoon fresh lemon juice
- 1 medium-sized tomato; chopped
- 1/2 teaspoon coarse salt
- 1/2 teaspoon ground black pepper
- 1/2 cup of fresh basil; roughly chopped

Directions:

1. Add the olive oil to an Air Fryer baking pan.
2. Make sure to tilt the pan to spread the oil evenly.
3. Simply combine the remaining ingredients; except for the basil leaves, whisk well until everything is well incorporated.
4. Cook in the preheated Air Fryer for 8 to 12 minutes at 280 - degrees Fahrenheit.
5. Garnish with fresh basil leaves.
6. Serve warm with a dollop of sour cream if desired.

Lemony Flounder Fillets

Preparation Time: 17 minutes

Servings: 2

Ingredients:

- 2 flounder fillets; boneless
- 2 garlic cloves; minced
- 2 tbsp. olive oil

- 2 tsp. coconut aminos
- 2 tbsp. lemon juice
- ½ tsp. stevia
- A pinch of salt and black pepper

Directions:

1. In a pan that fits your air fryer, mix all the ingredients, toss, introduce in the fryer and cook at 390 °F for 12 minutes. Divide into bowls and serve.

Nutrition:

Calories: 251; Fat: 13g; Fiber: 3g; Carbs: 5g; Protein: 10g

Garlic Lemon Shrimp

Preparation Time: 11 minutes

Servings: 2

Ingredients:

- 8 oz. medium shelled and deveined shrimp
- 2 tbsp. unsalted butter; melted.
- 1 medium lemon.

- ½ tsp. minced garlic
- ½ tsp. Old Bay seasoning

Directions:

1. Zest lemon and then cut in half. Place shrimp in a large bowl and squeeze juice from ½ lemon on top of them.
2. Add lemon zest to bowl along with remaining ingredients. Toss shrimp until fully coated
3. Pour bowl contents into 6-inch round baking dish. Place into the air fryer basket.
4. Adjust the temperature to 400 Degrees F and set the timer for 6 minutes. Shrimp will be bright pink when fully cooked. Serve warm with pan sauce.

Nutrition:

Calories: 190; Protein: 16.4g; Fiber: 0.4g; Fat: 11.8g; Carbs: 2.9g

E-Z Catfish

Preparation time: 15 minutes

Servings: 3

Ingredients:

- Olive oil: 1 tbsp.
- Seasoned fish fry: .25 cup
- Catfish fillets: 4

Directions:

1. Prepare the fryer to 400º Fahrenheit.
2. First, rinse the fish, and pat dry with a paper towel.
3. Dump the seasoning into a large zip-type baggie. Add the fish and shake to cover each fillet. Spray with a spritz of cooking oil spray. Add to the basket.
4. Set the timer for ten minutes. Flip, and reset the timer for ten more minutes. Flip once more and cook for two to three minutes.
5. Once it reaches the desired crispiness, transfer to a plate to serve.

Salmon Croquettes

Preparation time: 20 minutes

Servings: 4

Ingredients:

- Red salmon: 1 lb. can
- Breadcrumbs: 1 cup
- Eggs: 2
- Chopped parsley: half of 1 bunch

- Vegetable oil: .33 cup

Directions:
1. Set the Air Fryer at 392º Fahrenheit.
2. Drain and mash the salmon. Whisk and add the eggs and parsley.
3. In another dish, mix the breadcrumbs and oil.
4. Prepare 16 croquettes using the breadcrumb mixture.
5. Arrange in the preheated fryer basket for seven minutes.
6. Serve.

Peas and Cod Fillets

Preparation Time: 20 Minutes

Servings: 4

Ingredients:

- 4 cod fillets; boneless
- 2 cups peas
- 1/2 tsp. sweet paprika
- 1/2 tsp. oregano; dried
- 2 tbsp. parsley; chopped

- 2 garlic cloves; minced
- 4 tbsp. wine
- Salt and pepper to the taste

Directions:

1. In your food processor mix garlic with parsley, salt, pepper, oregano, paprika and wine and blend well.
2. Rub fish with half of this mix, place in your air fryer and cook at 360 °F, for 10 minutes
3. Meanwhile, put peas in a pot, add water to cover, add salt, bring to a boil over medium-high heat, cook for 10 minutes; drain and divide among plates. Also divide fish on plates, spread the rest of the herb dressing all over and serve

Sea Bass Paella

Preparation Time: 35 minutes

Servings: 4

Ingredients:

- 1 lb. sea bass fillets; cubed
- 6 scallops
- 1 red bell pepper; deseeded and chopped.
- 8 shrimp; peeled and deveined

- 2 oz. peas
- 5 oz. wild rice
- 14 oz. dry white wine
- 3½ oz. chicken stock
- A drizzle of olive oil
- Salt and black pepper to taste

Directions:

1. In a heatproof dish that fits your air fryer, place all the ingredients and toss
2. Place the dish in your air fryer and cook at 380°F and cook for 25 minutes, stirring halfway. Divide between plates and serve.

Hawaiian Salmon Recipe

Preparation Time: 20 Minutes

Servings: 2

Ingredients:

- 2 medium salmon fillets; boneless
- 1/2 tsp. ginger; grated
- 20-ounce canned pineapple pieces and juice
- 2 tsp. garlic powder
- 1 tsp. onion powder

- 1 tbsp. balsamic vinegar
- Salt and black pepper to the taste

Directions:

1. Season salmon with garlic powder, onion powder, salt and black pepper, rub well, transfer to a heat proof dish that fits your air fryer, add ginger and pineapple chunks and toss them really gently
2. Drizzle the vinegar all over, put in your air fryer and cook at 350 °F, for 10 minutes. Divide everything on plates and serve

Mussels Bowls

Preparation Time: 18 minutes

Servings: 4

Ingredients:

- 2 lbs. mussels; scrubbed
- 1 yellow onion; chopped.
- 8 oz. spicy sausage; chopped.
- 1 tbsp. olive oil
- 12 oz. black beer
- 1 tbsp. paprika

Directions:

1. Combine all the ingredients in a pan that fits your air fryer
2. Place the pan in the air fryer and cook at 400°F for 12 minutes. Divide the mussels into bowls, serve and enjoy!

Devil Chicken

Preparation time: 10-20,

Cooking time: 45-60;

Serve: 4

Ingredients:

- 1 kg of whole chicken
- Black pepper to taste

- Salt to taste
- Chili pepper

Direction:

1. Thoroughly clean the chicken and cut it along the white. Flatten it well on the work surface and then massage with oil and spices.
2. Cook the chicken for 35 minutes at 200 °C.
3. Turn the chicken and cook another 25 minutes.

Nutrition:

Calories 429.7, Fat 17.3 g, Carbohydrate 19.5 g, Sugars5.1 g, Protein51.1 g, Cholesterol 155.0 mg

Citrus Turkey Legs

Preparation Time: 15 minutes

Cooking Time: 30 minutes

Servings: 2

Ingredients:

- 2 turkey legs
- 1 tablespoon fresh rosemary, minced
- 2 garlic cloves, minced
- 1 teaspoon fresh lime zest, finely grated
- 2 tablespoons olive oil
- 1 tablespoon fresh lime juice
- Salt and black pepper, as required

Directions:

1. Preheat the Air fryer to 350 degrees F and grease an Air fryer basket.
2. Mix the garlic, rosemary, lime zest, oil, lime juice, salt, and black pepper in a bowl.

3. Coat the turkey legs with the marinade and refrigerate to marinate for about 8 hours.
4. Arrange the turkey legs into the Air Fryer basket and cook for about 30 minutes, flipping once in between.
5. Dish out the turkey legs into serving plates.

Nutrition:

Calories: 458, Fat: 29.5g, Carbohydrates: 2.3g, Sugar: 0.1g, Protein: 44.6g, Sodium: 247mg

Delightful Turkey Wings

Preparation Time: 10 minutes

Cooking Time: 26 minutes

Servings: 4

Ingredients:

- 4 tablespoons chicken rub
- 2 pounds turkey wings
- 3 tablespoons olive oil

Directions:

1. Preheat the Air fryer to 380 degrees F and grease an Air fryer basket.
2. Mix the turkey wings, chicken rub, and olive oil in a bowl until well combined.
3. Arrange the turkey wings into the Air fryer basket and cook for about 26 minutes, flipping once in between.
4. Dish out the turkey wings in a platter and serve hot.

Nutrition:

Calories: 204, Fat: 15.5g, Carbohydrates: 3g, Sugar: 0g, Protein: 12g, Sodium: 465mg

Chicken and Peppercorns

Preparation Time: 25 minutes

Servings: 4

Ingredients:

- 8 chicken thighs; boneless
- 1 tsp. black peppercorns
- 1/2 cup soy sauce
- 1/2 cup balsamic vinegar
- 4 garlic cloves; minced
- Salt and black pepper to taste

Directions:

1. In a pan that fits your air fryer; mix the chicken with all the other ingredients and toss
2. Place the pan in the fryer and cook at 380 °F for 20 minutes. Divide everything between plates and serve.

Garlic Chicken

Preparation Time: 10 minutes

Cooking Time: 32 minutes

Serve: 4

Ingredients:

- 2 lbs chicken drumsticks
- 9 garlic cloves, sliced
- 1 fresh lemon juice

- 2 tbsp parsley, chopped
- 4 tbsp butter, melted
- 2 tbsp olive oil
- Pepper
- Salt

Directions:

1. Preheat the air fryer to 400 °F.
2. Add all ingredients into the large mixing bowl and toss well.
3. Transfer chicken wings into the air fryer basket and cook for 32 minutes. Toss halfway through.
4. Serve and enjoy.

Nutrition:

Calories 560, Fat 31 g, Carbohydrates 3 g, Sugar 0.4 g, Protein 63 g, Cholesterol 230 mg

Chicken Fried Rice

Cooking Time: 20 minutes

Servings: 3

Ingredients:

- 1 cup chicken; cooked and diced
- 1 cup frozen peas and carrots
- 3 cups white rice; cooked
- 1/2 cup onion; diced
- 1 tbsp. vegetable oil
- 6 tbsp. soy sauce

Directions:

1. Place white rice into the mixing bowl, adding the vegetable oil and the soy sauce. Mix thoroughly.
2. Then, add the frozen peas and carrots, diced onions and diced chicken. Mix thoroughly once more
3. Pour the rice mixture into the nonstick pan and place in air fryer. Cook at 360 °F for 20 minutes. Once done, remove and serve.

Chicken Drumsticks

Cooking Time: 20 minutes

Servings: 4

Ingredients:

- 8 chicken drumsticks
- 1 large egg; lightly beaten.
- 1/3 cup oats
- 1/3 cup cauliflower

- 1 tsp. cayenne pepper
- 2 tbsp. thyme
- 2 tbsp. oregano
- 2 tbsp. mustard powder
- 3 tbsp. coconut milk
- Salt and pepper to taste

Directions:

1. Preheat your oven to 350 °F. Season chicken drumsticks with salt and pepper. Rub coconut milk all over chicken drumsticks
2. Add cayenne pepper, mustard powder, oregano, oats, thyme and cauliflower into the food processor and mix until you have a consistency of breadcrumbs. In a small bowl, add beaten egg
3. Dip the chicken into the breadcrumbs mixture then into egg and dip again into breadcrumbs. Place coated chicken drumsticks inside air fryer and cook for 20 minutes. Serve hot.

Bacon Wrapped Herb Chicken

Cooking Time: 15 minutes

Servings: 6

Ingredients:

- 1 chicken breast; cut into 6 pieces
- 1 tbsp. soft cheese
- 6 slices of bacon
- 1/2 tsp. parsley; dried.
- 1/2 tsp. paprika
- 1/2 tsp. basil; dried.
- Salt and pepper to taste

Directions:

1. In a bowl, mix basil, parsley, salt, pepper and paprika. Place the bacon slices on a dish and spread them with soft cheese
2. Place the chicken pieces into basil mix and cover with seasoning. Place the chicken pieces on top of bacon slices. Roll up and secure with toothpick.
3. Place into air fryer and cook at 350 °F and cook for 15 minutes

Lamb Stew

Preparation Time: 10 minutes

Cooking Time: 35 minutes

Servings: 5-6

Ingredients:

- 2 lbs of diced lamb stew meat
- 4 Medium carrots
- 1 Large acorn squash
- 2 Small yellow onions
- 2 Rosemary Sprigs.
- 1 bay leaf
- 6 sliced or minced cloves of garlic
- 3 Tbsp of broth or water
- ¼ Tbsp of sp salt (Adjust it to taste)

Directions:

1. Start by peeling and seeding, then cubing your acorn squash. You can use a nice trick which is to microwave the squash for 2 minutes.

2. Slice the carrots into quite thick circles.
3. Peel your onions and cut it into halves; then slice it into the shape of half-moons.
4. Now, place all of your ingredients in the Air fryer and set the feature Soup/ Stew button.
5. Lock the lid and set the timer to 35 minutes.
6. When the timer goes off; release the steam and pressure before opening the lid.
7. Serve and enjoy your stew.

Nutrition:

Calories – 332.7 Protein – 28.9 g. Fat – 6.9 g. Carbs – 38.9 g.

Herbed Lamb Chops

Preparation Time: 10 minutes

Cooking Time: 7 minutes

Servings: 2

Ingredients:

- 4: 4-ounceslamb chops
- 1 tablespoon fresh lemon juice
- 1 teaspoon dried rosemary
- 1 tablespoon olive oil
- 1 teaspoon dried thyme
- 1 teaspoon dried oregano
- ½ teaspoon ground cumin
- ½ teaspoon ground coriander
- Salt and black pepper, to taste

Directions:

1. Preheat the Air fryer to 390 degrees F and grease an Air fryer basket.

2. Mix the lemon juice, oil, herbs, and spices in a large bowl.
3. Coat the chops generously with the herb mixture and refrigerate to marinate for about 1 hour.
4. Arrange the chops in the Air fryer basket and cook for about 7 minutes, flipping once in between.
5. Dish out the lamb chops in a platter and serve hot.

Nutrition:

Calories: 491, Fat: 24g, Carbohydrates: 1.6g, Sugar: 0.2g, Protein: 64g, Sodium: 253mg

Veggie Stuffed Beef Rolls

Preparation Time: 20 minutes

Cooking Time: 14 minutes

Servings: 6

Ingredients:

- 6 Provolone cheese slices
- 2 pounds beef flank steak, pounded to 1/8-inch thickness
- 3-ounce roasted red bell peppers
- ¾ cup fresh baby spinach
- 3 tablespoons prepared pesto
- Salt and black pepper, to taste

Directions:

1. Preheat the Air fryer to 400 degrees F and grease an Air fryer basket.
2. Place the steak onto a smooth surface and spread evenly with pesto.

3. Top with the cheese slices, red peppers and spinach.
4. Roll up the steak tightly around the filling and secure with the toothpicks.
5. Arrange the roll in the Air fryer basket and cook for about 14 minutes, flipping once in between.
6. Dish out in a platter and serve warm.

Nutrition:

Calories: 447, Fats: 23.4g, Carbohydrates: 1.8g, Sugar: 0.6g, Proteins: 53.2g, Sodium: 472mg

Roasted Lamb

Preparation Time: 15 minutes

Cooking Time: 1 hour 30 minutes

Servings: 4

Ingredients:

- 1 tablespoon dried rosemary
- 2½ pounds half lamb leg roast, slits carved
- 2 garlic cloves, sliced into smaller slithers

- 1 tablespoon olive oil
- Cracked Himalayan rock salt and cracked peppercorns to taste

Directions:

1. Preheat the Air fryer to 400 degrees F and grease an Air fryer basket.
2. Insert the garlic slithers in the slits and brush with rosemary, oil, salt, and black pepper.
3. Arrange the lamb in the Air fryer basket and cook for about 15 minutes.
4. Set the Air fryer to 350 degrees F on the Roast mode and cook for 1 hour and 15 minutes.
5. Dish out the lamb chops and serve hot.

Nutrition:

Calories: 246, Fat: 7.4g, Carbohydrates: 9.4g, Sugar: 6.5g, Protein: 37.2g, Sodium: 353mg

Chinese Style Beef

Preparation Time: 25 minutes

Servings: 4

Ingredients:

- 1 lb. beef stew meat; cut into strips
- 1/4 cup sesame seeds; toasted
- 5 garlic cloves; minced
- 1 cup soy sauce
- 1 cup green onion; chopped
- Black pepper to taste

Directions:

1. In a pan that fits your air fryer, place all ingredients and mix well
2. Place the pan in the fryer and cook at 390 °F for 20 minutes. Divide everything into bowls and serve

Lamb and Beans

Preparation Time: 35 minutes

Servings: 4

Ingredients:

- 3 oz. canned kidney beans; drained
- 8 oz. lamb loin; cubed
- 1 tbsp. ginger; grated
- 3 tbsp. soy sauce

- 1 garlic clove; minced
- 1/2 tbsp. olive oil
- 1 yellow onion; sliced
- 1 carrot; chopped.
- Salt and black pepper to taste

Directions:

1. In baking dish that fits your air fryer, place all of the ingredients and mix well.
2. Place the dish in the fryer and cook at 390 °F for 30 minutes. Divide everything into bowls and serve

Simple Stuffed Tomatoes

Preparation Time: 10 minutes

Cooking duration: 15 minutes

Servings: 4

Ingredients:

- 4 tomatoes, tops cut off and pulp scooped and chopped Salt and black pepper to the taste
- 1 tablespoon butter
- 1 yellow onion, chopped
- 2 tablespoons celery, chopped
- ½ cup mushrooms, chopped
- 1 tablespoon bread crumbs
- 1 cup cottage cheese
- ¼ teaspoon caraway seeds
- 1 tablespoon parsley, chopped

Directions:

1. Heat up a pan with the butter over medium heat, melt it, add onion and celery, stir and cook for 3 minutes.

2. Add tomato pulp and mushrooms, stir and cook for 1 minute more.
3. Add salt, pepper, crumbled bread, cheese, caraway seeds and parsley, stir, cook for 4 minutes more and take off heat.
4. Stuff tomatoes with this mix, place them in your air fryer and cook at 350 °F for 8 minutes.
5. Divide stuffed tomatoes on plates and serve.

Nutrition:

Calories: 150; Fat: 4g; Fiber: 2g; Carbs: 4g; Protein: 5g

Herbed Veggies Combo

Preparation Time: 15 minutes

Cooking Time: 35 minutes

Servings: 4

Ingredients:

- ½ pound carrots, peeled and sliced
- 1 pound yellow squash, sliced
- ½ tablespoon fresh basil, chopped
- ½ tablespoon tarragon leaves, chopped
- 1 pound zucchini, sliced
- 6 teaspoons olive oil, divided
- Salt and ground white pepper, to taste

Directions:

1. Preheat the Air fryer to 400 degrees F and grease an Air fryer basket.
2. Mix two teaspoons of oil and carrot slices in a bowl.

3. Arrange the carrot slices in the Air fryer basket and cook for about 5 minutes.
4. Mix the remaining oil, yellow squash, zucchini, salt, and white pepper in a large bowl and toss to coat well.
5. Transfer the zucchini mixture into air fryer basket with carrots and cook for about 30 minutes, tossing twice in between.
6. Dish out in a bowl and sprinkle with the herbs to serve.

Nutrition:

Calories: 120, Fat: 7.4g, Carbohydrates: 13.3g, Sugar: 6.7g, Protein: 3.3g, Sodium: 101mg

Couscous Stuffed Tomatoes

Preparation Time: 10 minutes

Cooking Time: 25 minutes

Servings: 4

Ingredients:

- 4 tomatoes, tops and seeds removed
- 1 parsnip, peeled and finely chopped
- 1½ cups couscous
- 1 cup mushrooms, chopped
- 1 teaspoon olive oil
- 1 garlic clove, minced
- 1 tablespoon mirin sauce

Directions:

1. Preheat the Air fryer to 355 degrees F and grease an Air fryer basket.
2. Heat olive oil in a skillet on low heat and add parsnips, mushrooms and garlic.

3. Cook for about 5 minutes and stir in the mirin sauce and couscous.
4. Stuff the couscous mixture into the tomatoes and arrange into the Air fryer basket.
5. Cook for about 20 minutes and dish out to serve warm.

Nutrition:

Calories: 361, Fat: 2g, Carbohydrates: 75.5g, Sugar: 5.1g, Protein: 10.4g, Sodium: 37mg

Tofu with Veggies

Preparation Time: 25 minutes

Cooking Time: 22 minutes

Servings: 3

Ingredients:

- ½: 14-ouncesblock firm tofu, pressed and crumbled

- ½ cup frozen peas
- 3 cups cauliflower rice
- 1 cup carrot, peeled and chopped
- ½ cup broccoli, finely chopped
- 4 tablespoons low-sodium soy sauce, divided
- 1 teaspoon ground turmeric
- 1 tablespoon fresh ginger, minced
- 2 garlic cloves, minced
- 1 tablespoon rice vinegar
- 1½ teaspoons sesame oil, toasted

Directions:

1. Preheat the Air fryer to 370 degrees F and grease an Air fryer pan.
2. Mix the tofu, carrot, onion, 2 tablespoons of soy sauce, and turmeric in a bowl.
3. Transfer the tofu mixture into the Air fryer basket and cook for about 10 minutes.
4. Meanwhile, mix the cauliflower rice, broccoli, peas, ginger, garlic, vinegar, sesame oil, and remaining soy sauce in a bowl.

5. Stir in the cauliflower rice into the Air fryer pan and cook for about 12 minutes.
6. Dish out the tofu mixture onto serving plates and serve hot.

Nutrition:

Calories: 162, Fat: 5.5g, Carbohydrates: 20.4g, Sugar: 8.3g, Protein: 11.4g, Sodium: 1263mg

Cheese Stuffed Mushrooms

Servings: 4

Preparation Time: 15 minutes

Cooking Time: 8 minutes

Ingredients

- 4 fresh large mushrooms, stemmed and gills removed
- 2 garlic cloves, chopped
- ¼ cup Parmesan cheese, shredded
- 4 ounces cream cheese, softened
- 2 tablespoons white cheddar cheese, shredded
- 2 tablespoons sharp cheddar cheese, shredded
- 1 teaspoon Worcestershire sauce
- Salt and ground black pepper, as required

Directions:

1. In a bowl, mix well cream cheese, Parmesan, cheddar cheeses, Worcestershire sauce, garlic, salt, and black pepper.

2. Set the temperature of air fryer to 370 degrees F. Grease an air fryer basket.
3. Stuff each mushroom with the cheese mixture.
4. Arrange stuffed mushrooms into the prepared air fryer basket.
5. Air fry for about 8 minutes.
6. Remove from air fryer and transfer the mushrooms onto a serving platter.
7. Set aside to cool slightly.
8. Serve warm.

Nutrition:

Calories: 156, Carbohydrate: 2.6g, Protein: 6.5g, Fat: 13.6g, Sugar: 0.7g, Sodium: 267mg

Air fryer Mediterranean Lentil and Collard Soup

Preparation Time: 10 minutes

Cooking Time: 20 minutes

Servings: 6

Ingredients:

- 2 tablespoons of extra virgin olive oil
- 1 medium yellow onion, chopped
- 2 medium celery stocks, diced
- 3 garlic cloves, minced
- 2 teaspoons of ground cumin
- 1 1/2 cups brown lentils, rinsed in water
- 1 teaspoon of ground turmeric
- 4 cups of low-sodium vegetable broth
- 1 ¼ cup of water
- 2 carrots, peeled and diced
- 1 bay leaf
- 1 teaspoon himalayan salt
- ½ teaspoon of ground black pepper
- 3 collard leaves, cut into strips

- 1 teaspoon of lemon juice

Directions:

1. Set air fryer to saute, then add the olive oil, heat, and add onions and celery. Stir often for 5 minutes. Turn the air fryer off.
2. Stir in the garlic, cumin, and turmeric until combined.
3. Add broth, water, lentils, carrots, bay leaf, salt, and pepper. Lock the lid and close the valve. Fix to manual and cook on high pressure for 13 minutes.
4. After completion, quick release the pressure, carefully remove the lid and stir in collards and lemon juice.
5. Make sure to lock the lid and set to manual and cook for 2 more minutes on high. Quick-release the pressure, open the lid, and it's ready to serve.

Nutrition:

Calories – 127.9 Protein – 7.3 g. Fat – 0.8 g. Carbs – 25.9 g.

Air fryer Bean Soup

Preparation Time: 20 minutes

Cooking Time: 1 hour and 25 minutes

Servings: 6

Ingredients:

- 1 pound white beans
- 1 white onion, chopped
- 1 ¼ pound of beef shanks with bone
- 1 green bell pepper, chopped
- 2 carrots, chopped
- 4 tablespoons olive oil
- ½ teaspoon garlic, minced
- 2 tablespoons fresh parsley, chopped
- ½ tablespoon salt
- 1 can tomatoes, diced
- 1 liter water
- 3 bay leaves
- ½ teaspoon paprika

Directions:

1. Immerse beans in a bowl of cold water overnight.
2. Place the beef shanks and olive oil in air fryer and turn on saute setting. Brown on both sides
3. Remove the beans from water, and rinse. Add beans, diced tomatoes, paprika, bay leaves, and garlic.
4. Add water, close the lid, and cook on the manual high setting for 1 hour. Make sure the beans are soft, and if not, cook for another 30 minutes. Serve.

Nutrition:

Calories – 86 Protein – 2.8 g. Fat – 5 g. Carbs – 9.7 g.

Cheese and Leeks Dip

Preparation Time: 17 minutes

Servings: 6

Ingredients:

- 2 spring onions; minced
- 2 tbsp. butter; melted
- 4 leeks; sliced
- ¼ cup coconut cream
- 3 tbsp. coconut milk
- Salt and white pepper to the taste

Directions:

1. In a pan that fits your air fryer, mix all the ingredients and whisk them well.
2. Introduce the pan in the fryer and cook at 390°F for 12 minutes. Divide into bowls and serve

Nutrition:

Calories: 204; Fat: 12g; Fiber: 2g; Carbs: 4g; Protein: 14g

Mozzarella Sticks

Preparation Time: 1 hour 10 minutes

Servings: 12 sticks

Ingredients:

- 2 large eggs.
- 6: 1-oz.mozzarella string cheese sticks
- ½ oz. pork rinds, finely ground
- ½ cup grated Parmesan cheese.
- 1 tsp. dried parsley.

Directions:

1. Place mozzarella sticks on a cutting board and cut in half. Freeze 45 minutes or until firm. If freezing overnight, remove frozen sticks after 1 hour and place into an airtight zip-top storage bag and place back in freezer for future use.
2. Take a large bowl, mix Parmesan, ground pork rinds and parsley
3. Take a medium bowl, whisk eggs

4. Dip a frozen mozzarella stick into beaten eggs and then into Parmesan mixture to coat.
5. Repeat with the remaining sticks. Place mozzarella sticks into the air fryer basket.
6. Adjust the temperature to 400 Degrees F and set the timer for 10 minutes or until golden. Serve warm.

Nutrition:

Calories: 236; Protein: 19.2g; Fiber: 0.0g; Fat: 13.8g; Carbs: 4.7g

Sunflower Seeds Bread

Preparation Time: 15 minutes

Cooking Time: 18 minutes

Servings: 4

Ingredients:

- 2/3 cup whole wheat flour
- 1/3 cup sunflower seeds
- 2/3 cup plain flour
- 1 cup lukewarm water
- ½ sachet instant yeast
- 1 teaspoon salt

Directions:

1. Preheat the Air fryer to 390 degrees F and grease a cake pan.
2. Mix together flours, sunflower seeds, yeast and salt in a bowl.
3. Add water slowly and knead for about 5 minutes until a dough is formed.

4. Cover the dough with a plastic wrap and keep in warm place for about half an hour.
5. Arrange the dough into a cake pan and transfer into an Air fryer basket.
6. Cook for about 18 minutes and dish out to serve warm.

Nutrition:

Calories: 156, Fat: 2.4g, Carbohydrates: 28.5g, Sugar: 0.5g, Protein: 4.6g, Sodium: 582mg

Spiced Soy Curls

Preparation Time: 15 minutes

Cooking Time: 10 minutes

Servings: 2

Ingredients:

- 3 cups boiling water
- 4 ounces soy curls, soaked in boiling water for about 10 minutes and drained
- ¼ cup fine ground cornmeal
- 2 teaspoons Cajun seasoning
- ¼ cup nutritional yeast
- 1 teaspoon poultry seasoning
- Salt and ground white pepper, to taste

Directions:

1. Preheat the Air fryer to 385 °F and grease an Air fryer basket.
2. Mix together cornmeal, nutritional yeast, Cajun seasoning, poultry seasoning, salt and white pepper in a bowl.

3. Coat the soy curls generously with this mixture and arrange in the Air fryer basket.
4. Cook for about 10 minutes, flipping in between and dis out in a serving platter.

Nutrition:

Calories: 317, Fat: 10.2g, Carbohydrates: 30.8g, Sugar: 2g, Protein: 29.4g, Sodium: 145mg

Peanut Butter Cookies

Preparation Time: 10 minutes

Cooking Time: 5 minutes

Servings: 24

Ingredients:

- 1 egg, lightly beaten
- 1 cup creamy peanut butter
- 1 cup of sugar

Directions:

1. In a big bowl, combine sugar, egg, and peanut butter together until well mixed.
2. Spray air fryer oven tray with cooking spray.
3. Using ice cream scooper scoop out cookie onto the tray and flattened them using a fork.
4. Bake cookie at 350 °F for 5 minutes.
5. Cook remaining cookie batches using the same temperature.
6. Serve and enjoy.

Nutrition:

Calories – 97 Protein – 2.9 g.Fat – 5.6 g.Carbs – 10.5 g.

Coffee Cheesecakes Recipe

Preparation Time: 30 Minutes

Servings: 6

Ingredients:

For the cheesecakes:
- 3 eggs
- 2 tbsp. butter
- 3 tbsp. coffee
- 8-ounce cream cheese
- 1/3 cup sugar
- 1 tbsp. caramel syrup

For the frosting:
- 3 tbsp. caramel syrup
- 2 tbsp. sugar
- 8-ounce mascarpone cheese; soft
- 3 tbsp. butter

Directions:

1. In your blender, mix cream cheese with eggs, 2 tablespoon butter, coffee, 1 tablespoon caramel syrup and ⅓ cup sugar and pulse very well, spoon into a cupcakes pan that fits your air fryer, introduce in the fryer and cook at 320 °F and bake for 20 minutes.
2. Leave aside to cool down and then keep in the freezer for 3 hours. Meanwhile; in a bowl, mix 3 tablespoon butter with 3 tablespoon caramel syrup, 2 tablespoon sugar and mascarpone, blend well, spoon this over the cheesecakes and serve them

Ginger Cookies

Preparation Time: 10 minutes

Cooking time: 15 minutes

Servings: 12

Ingredients:

- 2 cups almond flour
- 1 cup swerve

- 1 egg
- ¼ cup butter, melted
- 2 teaspoons ginger, grated
- 1 teaspoon vanilla extract
- ¼ teaspoon nutmeg, ground
- ¼ teaspoon cinnamon powder

Directions:

1. In a bowl, mix all the Ingredients: and whisk well.
2. Spoon small balls out of this mix on a lined baking sheet that fits the air fryer lined with parchment paper and flatten them.
3. Put the sheet in the fryer and cook at 360 degrees F for 15 minutes.
4. Cool the cookies down and serve.

Nutrition:

Calories 220, fat 13, fiber 2, carbs 4, protein 3

Cherry-Choco Bars

Servings: 8

Cooking Time: 15 minutes

Ingredients

- ¼ teaspoon salt
- ½ cup almonds, sliced
- 1/3 cup honey
- ½ cup chia seeds
- ½ cup dark chocolate, chopped
- ½ cup dried cherries, chopped
- ½ cup prunes, pureed
- ½ cup quinoa, cooked
- ¾ cup almond butter
- 2 cups old-fashioned oats
- 2 tablespoon coconut oil

Directions:

1. Preheat the air fryer to 375 degrees F.

2. In a mixing bowl, combine the oats, quinoa, chia seeds, almond, cherries, and chocolate.
3. In a saucepan, heat the almond butter, honey, and coconut oil.
4. Pour the butter mixture over the dry mixture. Add salt and prunes.
5. Mix until well combined.
6. Pour over a baking dish that can fit inside the air fryer.
7. Cook for 15 minutes.
8. Let it cool for an hour before slicing into bars.

Nutrition:

Calories: 321; Carbohydrates: 35g; Protein: 7g; Fat: 17g

Notes

www.ingramcontent.com/pod-product-compliance
Lightning Source LLC
Chambersburg PA
CBHW070936080526
44589CB00013B/1525